A DORLING KINDERSLEY BOOK

Note to Parents

My First Look At Shopping is designed to help young children learn about the different types of shops and the goods they sell – whether we buy cakes from the baker's shop, or a kitten from the pet shop. It's a book for you and your child to share and enjoy – looking at the pages together, finding familiar objects, and learning and using new words.

Editors Andrea Pinnington, Charlotte Davies
Designer Heather Blackham
Managing Editor Jane Yorke
Senior Art Editor Mark Richards

Photography Steve Gorton
Additional Photography Mike Dunning, Dave King
Model Jack Richards
Series Consultant Neil Morris

Dorling Kindersley would like to thank Gaby Noble for the loan of Biggles the budgie.

First published in Great Britain in 1991
by Dorling Kindersley Limited,
9 Henrietta Street, London WC2E 8PS

Copyright © 1991 Dorling Kindersley Limited, London

All rights reserved. No part of this publication may be reproduced, stored in a retrieval system, or transmitted in any form or by any means, electronic, mechanical, photocopying, recording or otherwise, without the prior written permission of the copyright owner.

A CIP catalogue record for this book is available from the British Library.

ISBN 0-86318-606-8

Reproduced by Bright Arts, Hong Kong
Printed and bound in Italy by L.E.G.O.

MY · FIRST · LOOK · AT
Shopping

DK

DORLING KINDERSLEY
London • New York • Stuttgart

Going shopping

We need money to pay for the things we buy.

coins

piggy-bank

shopping basket

Greengrocer's shop

We buy fruit and vegetables at the greengrocer's shop.

oranges

apples

lemons and limes

Baker's shop

The baker sells bread and all kinds of cakes.

cake

croissants

gingerbread men

fruit tarts

Toy shop

We buy toys, games, and puzzles at the toy shop.

teddy bear

abacus

construction kit

Clothes shop

We can buy new things to wear at the clothes shop.

tee shirts

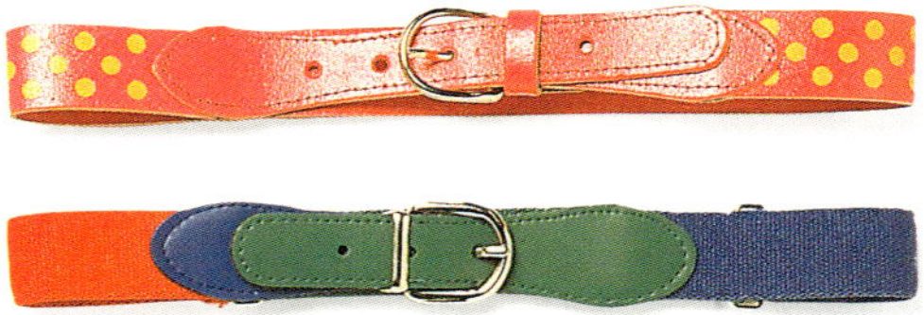

belts

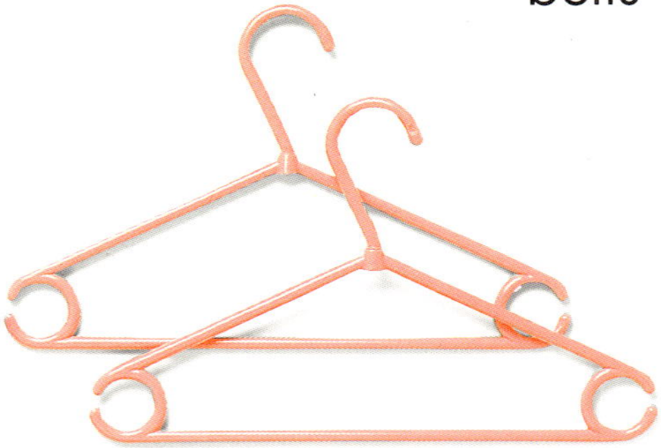

hangers

socks

Pet shop

The pet shop sells food and toys for our animals.

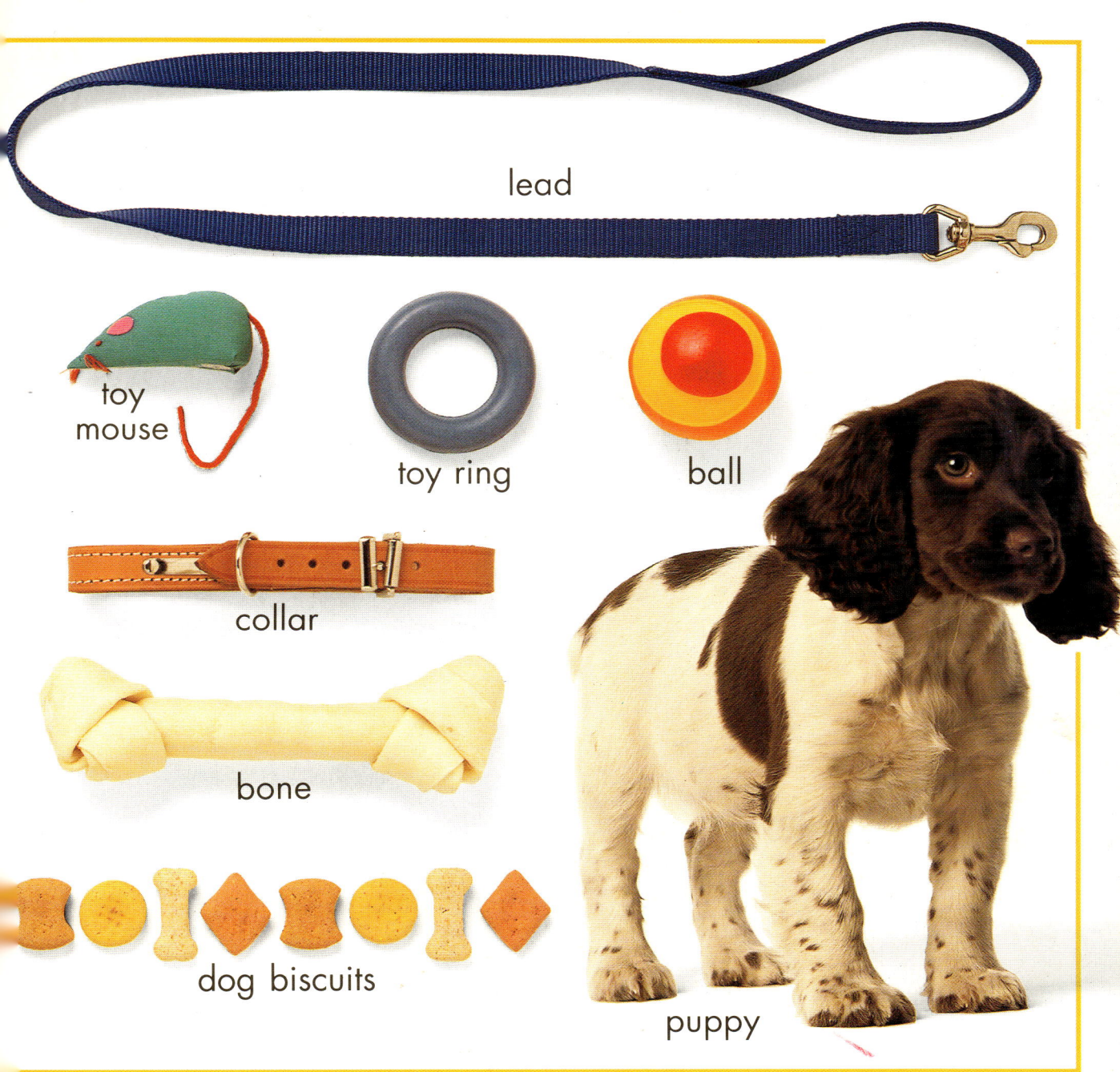

Stationery shop

We buy pens and paper from the stationer's.

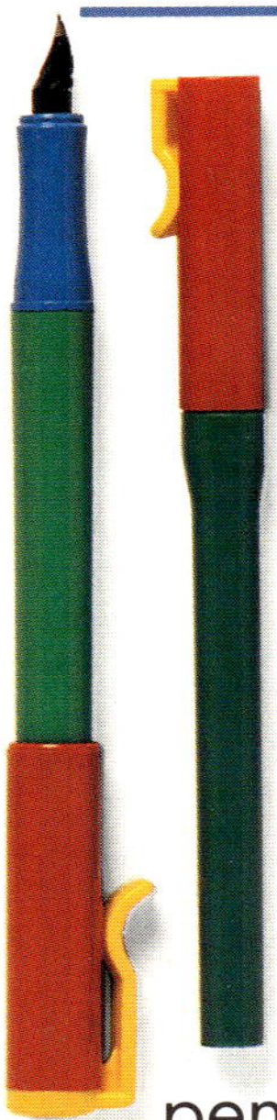

pens

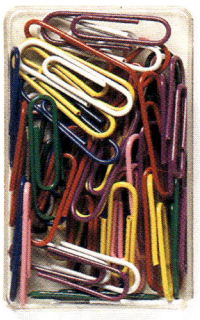
drawing pins

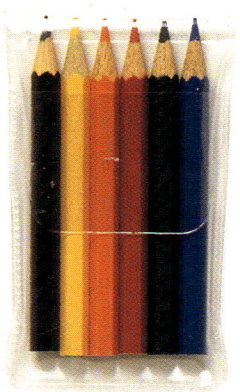
paper clips

coloured pencils

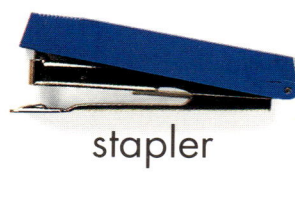
stapler

rubbers

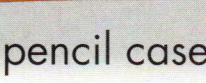
pencil case

string

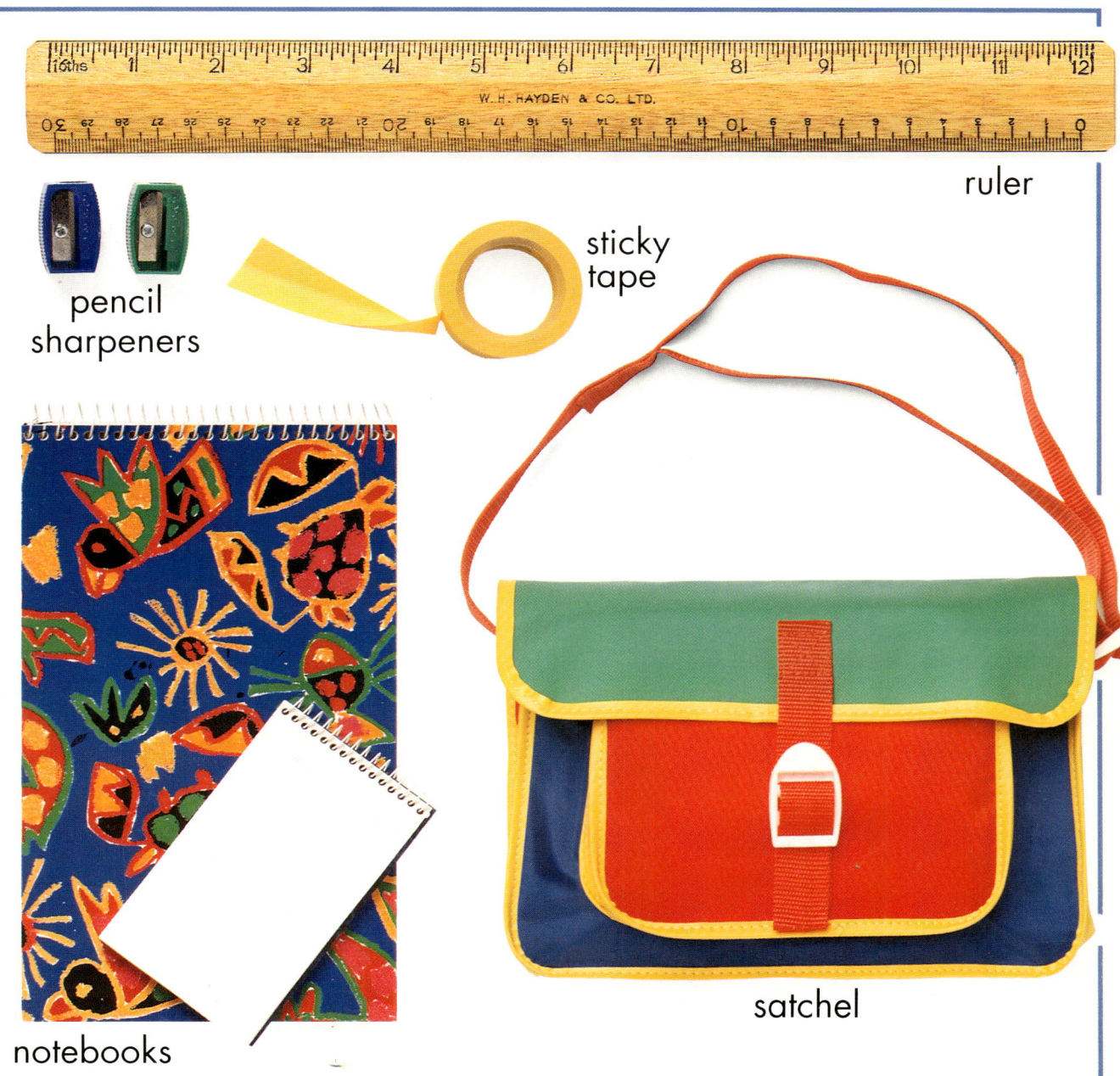